THE RIDE OF YOUR LIFE

choosing what drives you

I0345846

191 Bank Street
Burlington Vermont 05401

Also by Cinse Bonino:
Relationship Residue

Publisher's Cataloging-in-Publication data

Names: Bonino, Cinse, author.
Title: The Ride of your life : choosing what drives you Cinse Bonino.
Description: Burlington, VT: Onion River Press, 2018.
Identifiers: ISBN 978-0-9976458-3-5 (pbk.) | 978-0-9976458-4-2 (ebook) | LCCN 2017960724
Subjects: LCSH Fear. | Worry. | Self-actualization (Psychology) | BISAC SELF-HELP / Self-Management / General | SELF-HELP / Personal Growth / General
Classification: LCC BF575.F2 B66 2018 | DDC 248.4--dc23

©2017 Cinse Bonino ALL RIGHTS RESERVED

ABOUT THE BOOK

How often does fear influence your choices? Everyone gets tempted to allow fear to take charge of their lives when they shouldn't. If you are ready to kick fear out of the driver's seat this book can help. Learn how your fear convinces you to put it in charge of making decisions for you. Learn which of fear's lies are easiest for you to believe. Become familiar with your own particular version of fear. Realize how dwelling on things that happened in the past and worrying about what will or will not happen in the future can convince you to overreact in the present. Discover when to listen to fear and when to realize it's being a drama queen spouting worst-case scenarios. Develop the courage to kick fear to the curb once you understand that the opposite of failure isn't success, it's learning. Be kind to yourself as you begin to choose intelligence, experiential knowledge, intuition, and instinct as your primary drivers. Transform your life by choosing to listen to fear only when it's doing its job appropriately. Learn to use your fear as the helpful tool it can be instead of allowing it to carjack your connection to reality.

*for Richie P, my sweet boy,
who is more awake in this life
than anyone else I know*

CONTENTS

1	The Ride	11
2	The Wheedling	19
3	The Invitations	27
4	The Timeline	35
5	The Perfect Pictures	43
6	The Face-to-face	51
7	The Avoidance	57
8	The Set-up	63
9	The Rejection	71
10	The What if?	77

CHAPTER 1
The Ride

THE RIDE OF YOUR LIFE

Imagine life is a taxi ride. You are a passenger, riding shotgun up front next to the driver. You are not permitted to drive. You can look through the windshield to see where you are headed. You also can use the side view mirror to check out where you've been. You get to choose your driver, and you can switch drivers any time you want. The pool of available drivers for this metaphysical cab ride includes the various emotions, worldviews, innate and learned tendencies, and other lovely or disagreeable elements that comprise you. If you neglect or refuse to choose a driver, your subconscious will choose for you. Sometimes your subconscious will choose wisely by accurately assessing what's happening in the present. However, your subconscious often may make a harmful or regrettable choice if you are holding onto negative emotions from past events that mirror your current situation. Any misplaced optimism or panic on your part can also influence your subconscious to make unhelpful choices.

Once selected, your driver gets to choose how to handle any potholes, bumps, detours or roadblocks you encounter; and also decides how fast to go on the wide-open, smooth stretches of your journey. This can become problematic if fear is in the driver's seat when it shouldn't be. Fear is great in life-or-death situations, when you need a fight or flight response, or need to shake yourself out of feeling frozen or helpless. But fear shouldn't be trusted to drive during circumstances that don't fit these conditions. Fear should never be your designated, on-the-regular driver, or the default when you don't know what else to pick.

Fear, however, should always be with you on your ride. Fear is useful. It is a necessary tool. Just as pain informs you when something feels *off or wrong* in your body, fear lets you know when something feels *not quite right or horribly wrong in your life*. If you attempt to journey through life without fear – if you refuse to allow it to come along for the ride – fear will carjack your taxi and attempt to take you somewhere you really don't want to go. In other words if you fear your fear, you automatically put it in charge.

Fear will use every trick it can to convince you it is the perfect driver for almost any portion of your journey, because fear loves to be in charge. You and your fear have been together a long time and it has been paying attention. Fear knows all the steps to your particular, personalized dance of panic. It is also completely familiar with the rhythm and timing of your freak-outs. Fear knows which tricks will work because it knows *you*. Fear will act as if

THE RIDE OF YOUR LIFE 13

any past permission for it to take charge means it now has license to take over anytime it wants, even if this is not what you had intended. Fear always wants more: more time in the driver's seat; more attention from you; and more credit for saving your butt, even when it didn't actually rescue you. But you can't completely ignore fear. You need it. It's vital. Sometimes it actually does save your butt. So what can you do?

Respect fear as the useful tool it is and keep it in the trunk, available for when you need it. Learn when you should let it move to the backseat to whisper a legitimate warning in your ear. Pay attention when fear's warnings make sense to you but also recognize when fear is being a drama queen. Fear loves to talk about disaster. It relishes imagining worse-case scenarios. Try to separate the blockbuster-esque hype fear pitches your way from the small kernels of truth hiding in its messages of doom and destruction. Refuse to unconditionally allow fear to jump into the driver's seat just because it says it should, but at the same time, don't try to completely eject fear from your ride through life. You need your fear. You also need to take charge of deciding when to listen to your fear.

Assume you'll make mistakes. There will be times when you buy into false warnings. Don't be too hard on yourself. Fear knows all your buttons and the best way to push each one. Fear shows disaster previews designed especially for you, as in: *This message has been approved specifically to scare the hell out of you.* Other times you'll regret not paying more attention to what fear was trying to tell you, or you'll feel stupid for closing your ears to what you didn't want to admit was true. It's a learning curve, but don't worry, you'll be headed in the right direction. But be aware, success rates drop if you repeatedly let fear jump directly to the driver's seat anytime it mumbles from the trunk. Pay attention. Learn the tricks your fear uses to get you to believe inaccurate and overblown information. Learn how you convince yourself to ignore fear's helpful warnings, especially when you feel too afraid to listen.

Remember fear is a tool and that tools are not inherently scary. If you borrowed a friend's car and discovered a tire iron when you opened the trunk, you wouldn't start screaming. But freaking out would probably be a completely rational response if a huge human were brandishing that same tire iron and chasing you with malicious intent. Fear will invite you to believe that your negative feelings are too overwhelming for you to handle. It will assure you it can save you from having to face the feelings you want to avoid. Fear will try to convince you it will be able to turbo-drive your life-taxi away from

THE RIDE OF YOUR LIFE

everything that frightens you just as soon as you put it in charge. This does not make sense. Fear doesn't get rid of fear. Fear generates fear.

Be very clear about fear's place in your life. Don't let fear scare you into letting it be in charge. Do allow fear to come along for the ride in order to caution you when it suspects something isn't quite right. Permit it to suggest when it may be time for you to take an evasive action. Only allow fear to take the driver's seat for a few moments in life threatening or other extremely dangerous circumstances. Then make sure it quickly relinquishes the wheel to intelligence, experiential knowledge, intuition, or instinct. Be warned: fear will do almost anything to convince you to allow it to stay behind the wheel once it gets there. It will offer cascading images of potential, worst-case scenarios hoping to paralyze you with dread. Things often begin to feel as if they are happening in slow motion when we freeze in fright. This means you may not be aware of how long you are actually allowing fear to be in control of your journey. You don't have to be afraid of fear because you get to decide when to let it out of the trunk and when it has to go back. You also get to decide how you choose to respond when you hear what fear has to say. Pay attention when it gives you helpful information. Do some discovery when you find yourself questioning if fear is freaking out unnecessarily. Only listen to fear when it's actually doing its job correctly. Curb your fear when it becomes overzealous. Help your fear evolve into an appropriate and effective early-warning system, designed specifically for your life.

Remember: Most of the time fear should ride in the trunk.

CHAPTER 2
The Wheedling

THE RIDE OF YOUR LIFE

The more often you allow fear to be in control when it doesn't need to be, the faster it will develop a taste for dominating your world. It will veer from its actual job of pointing out things you should avoid and potentially dangerous situations that warrant further exploration. Instead it will begin to pour its vast energies into attempting to scare or entice you into habitually granting it control without question.

Fear has a wide repertoire of persuasion techniques it uses to convince you to give it permission to drive. One of these is the *this-looks-just-like-that-other-time* comparison. Fear will point out and then latch tenaciously onto a particular word or phrase uttered by someone in your life. It will insist these words are a sure sign a horrible incident from your past is about to be repeated. Fear may zero in instead on a tiny but familiar gesture someone makes or point out a particular facial expression or moment of silence. Regardless of what fear draws your attention to, it will aggressively steer you away from taking even a moment to uncover the actual meaning behind someone's words or actions. Fear will tell you there's no time to explore because you are in an emergency situation rapidly working its way toward becoming a tragedy. This is how fear invites you to become completely freaked out by any similarities to former negative events in your life. If you buy into fear's analysis of the situation you may find yourself eagerly handing over control so fear can save you. This is fear's implied promise: *If you put fear in control you will no longer need to be afraid because fear will rescue you.*

The truth is, fear is a diagnostician not a surgeon. It can do some stopgap initial aid in a true emergency, but then it's time to bring in intelligence, experiential knowledge, intuition, and instinct. These are your experts who have greater skills to offer. Individually or working together they: 1) consider causality – *Why is this happening right here and right now?*; 2) understand subtle and important distinctions and differences between one situation and another – *How is this the same, yet potentially different from what happened before?*; 3) know effective treatment and recovery protocols – *Slow down, take a breath, check this out;* and 4) are familiar with your emotional and experiential histories – *You know you almost always overreact to those particular words.* Once your experts show up, fear usually ends up back in the trunk. Fear knows it has to work fast to get you to wholeheartedly believe its gloom and doom predictions. It prays you won't realize its job of alerting you to a potential problem is over and that it's now time for you to call in your experts.

THE RIDE OF YOUR LIFE

Be suspicious if your fear only seems to have one setting, especially if it's DEFCON 1. A defense readiness condition (DEFCON) of 1 portends total global annihilation, as in: utter destruction is a distinct possibility. If fear can convince you a situation merits high-alert status it becomes far easier to convince you there is no time to hesitate, no time to decide for yourself how dangerous or potentially hazardous things currently are. If you are convinced all may be lost if you don't act NOW, if you have no idea what to do to save yourself, fear starts to look like a hero. Once you push the panic button and cover your ears to protect yourself from the cacophony of warning alarms going off in your head, giving fear permission to drive is just a formality. You've already put fear behind the wheel.

Another persuasion technique fear often uses is the *I-don't-know-what's-going-on-so-something-terrible-is-probably-going-to-happen* pitch. Fear's first method is about convincing you to automatically be afraid of whatever looks or sounds familiar in an achingly unpleasant and undesired way. This second technique instead capitalizes on something being unfamiliar, unknown, or only partially in focus. Fear will helpfully fill in the blanks with numerous dreadful possibilities. It will ask you: *What if it's horrible? uncontrollable? overwhelming? life-altering? insurmountable?*

unsurvivable?

The first several words fear offers to you may be slightly different from those listed above because fear knows which words most effectively drop you into panic mode. However, that last word, *unsurvivable*, is the word everyone's fear labors to get their particular person to consider. Why? Because *unsurvivable* is the worst possible outcome. It means you will not survive. Your logical brain most likely realizes that unless you are facing a tsunami-level incident you probably are going to survive. Your logical brain also understands the situation is in no way life ending even while recognizing the potential for things to become unpleasant or difficult, but fear has learned to bypass our logical brains. Everyone panics when they feel threatened. Those who survive difficult situations share the tendency to give into panic for a shorter period of time, even if they keep a small portion of panic throbbing in the background. These people intentionally choose to then move beyond panic, beyond fear, and to use: logic, experiential knowledge, intuition, and possibly instinct to meet whatever challenges they face. It is impossible to think when you stay in panic mode. This is as true emotionally as it would be if you were in the ocean surrounded by actual sharks.

Thinking requires you to slow down. Even if you are capable of rapidly assessing your situation and then quickly devising a solution, you must first slow down to disengage yourself from complete panic. Fear knows this. Fear will fan your terror. It will use all its tricks to convince you that even things as commonplace as embarrassment and uncertainty have the potential to end us.

Remember: Fear can be such a liar.

CHAPTER 3
The Invitations

THE RIDE OF YOUR LIFE

Fear uses its knowledge of the secret things that can instantly terrify you to convince you to put it in control. However, fear realizes even a small glimpse of the truth has the potential to diminish your imagined terrors, so it cunningly mislabels whatever is happening and maneuvers you away from logic and reason. Fear understands that the minute you begin to question the truth of what it tells you, it begins to lose control. Fear is tricky. It will appear to invite you to assess what is happening but will skillfully steer you toward noticing only the evidence that seems to confirm its version of what is taking place.

Imagine you're walking briskly down the sidewalk in town on your way to a meeting and spot a friend you haven't seen for quite some time. After saying hello and mentioning how long it's been since you last spent time together, you each promise to get back in touch soon. As you begin to turn to walk toward the direction of your appointment, you catch a glimpse of an odd look on your friend's face. You turn back to look more carefully but your friend has already turned and begun to walk away. It didn't appear to be an angry or disgusted look, but it wasn't an overtly friendly look either.

Then fear gets busy constructing an alternate reality. It tells you your friend's expression means they were thinking something negative about you. If the person were someone significant in your life instead of a friend you hadn't seen for some time, say a manager or a romantic partner, it might be even more difficult to refuse fear's invitation to believe the glance was negative. Fear may suggest this significant person believes you aren't up to standard or thinks you are a complete and utter failure. The greater the impact this person has on our work, our hearts, or any other major area of our lives, the more likely we are to accept fear's invitation to believe the worst about that one little glance.

Fear invites us to replay the encounter in our minds, to examine and reexamine what occurred. We are prompted to ask ourselves questions such as: *Did the person's tone sound a little off? Did their body language seem a little distant? Were their seemingly polite words masking discontent?* Fear then guides us to start thinking about the last time we saw this person. We are invited once again to replay the person's words and actions to look for hidden negative messages we may have missed. *Was there a foreshadowing of today's non-friendly look? Was there any indication the person was harboring a grudge or judging us in some way?*

At this point fear begins to do some of its best

THE RIDE OF YOUR LIFE

work. It will combine our memories of what this person said or did in the past with that one indecipherable glance to convince us our greatest fears about this person's opinion of us are true. Normally it would be quite a stretch to believe the validity of the misconstrued evidence fear offers us, but it's easier to trust fear's distorted logic when we're already well on our way to relabeling almost everything as negative. Besides, fear is probably whispering things such as: *What if this person really is thinking something horrible about you and you miss it? You'll end up looking like a fool.*

This all makes us more inclined to accept fear's invitation to feel the deeply negative emotions associated with being unfairly judged or rejected. Is it really possible to give fear the power to use one small, difficult-to-decipher glance to take us all the way to this deeply negative place? Yes it is. And if you give fear enough leeway it won't stop there. Fear will invite you to feel like a victim and encourage you to cast your glancing acquaintance in the role of villain. It will urge you to share these feelings and judgments with others, helpfully pointing you toward those who will readily agree with your assessment of the situation and fuel your growing anger towards the glancer. These individuals probably believe they are being supportive when they tell you: *You don't deserve to* be treated *that* way, and then encourage you to do everything in your power to make sure this villain never gets to victimize you or anyone else again.

You may feel vindicated by this so-called support and use it to construct a form of self-protective animosity towards the glancer. You and your supporters may begin to feel virtuous as you spread the word about the glancer's villainous acts to spare others from the same fate. All of this does nothing to quell the anxiety you began to feel when you first noticed that difficult to decipher glance, but it does give all the negativity somewhere to go. It channels it into anger, hatred, and blame. Secretly, you may also worry you are unlovable or unworthy but you'd really rather not go down that road; blaming the glancer keeps you away from those kinds of thoughts.

Since this is only an imaginary scenario and we aren't actually mired in all these negative thoughts, let's step back and theorize about what may have been going on in the glancer's mind during the moment that sparked all this turmoil. Let's start with the best-case scenario. The glancer had a benign or trivial reason for that look. Maybe it was indigestion or an urgent need to pee combined with a lack of information about where to find a restroom quickly without being late for their appointment. Or maybe they were simply a little anxious about what was going to transpire during their appointment. What if you villainized this person because they had to pee? The glance wasn't overtly negative; it was simply hard to read. It's probably just as likely to have been something harmless as to have been the horrific situation fear invited you to believe it was. How would you feel if you discovered it was basically nothing? Probably a little foolish about how rapidly your anger rose to the frenzy point, and maybe pretty guilty for how willing you were to instantly misjudge this person and then trash their reputation without investigating fear's claims.

Now, let's imagine the person actually was thinking about voicing a concern they had about their relationship with you. What if they weren't angry with you or judging you but rather were confused or hurt? What if they were contemplating talking to you about this at a later date when you both weren't in such a hurry? Would any part of the over-the-top, negative reaction fear persuaded you to feel be helpful? Would it support you to be open to hear and understand what the glancer would try to say? Would it allow you to be vulnerable enough to connect with your friend in an authentic way? I smell burning bridges; do you?

Finally, what if this really was the worst-case scenario fear described to you? What if this person thinks you are unworthy or lacking? What if they think you are a waste of air? Maybe they are a jerk and their opinion isn't based on who you are but on their own fears. Maybe a small part of what they think may actually be helpful for you to hear. Maybe they have some insight you could use. Maybe not. Either way, would fear's counsel have helped you if any of this were true? Not really. If the person is a jerk, villainizing them doesn't protect you. Recognizing they are acting out of their own anger and fear can help you to feel compassion for them AND to draw some very clear boundaries for yourself. You may choose to no longer associate with them. You may decide to reject their judgments of you, or you may decide to first consider if there are any helpful bits you want to take with you. Both of these things would be very difficult to do if you were awash in hatred and blame. It's quite possible fear's suggested response would complicate or escalate any potential scenario.

Remember: Fear likes to cause trouble.

CHAPTER 4
The Timeline

THE RIDE OF YOUR LIFE

According to Einstein's theories of relativity, now is simply a point that exists at a particular distance from the things that happened in our past, behind us, and from those yet to occur in our future, up ahead of us. Many world religions and wellness groups view now as where we should put our attention. They advise us to *live in the now* and to be present to what is happening at any given moment in our lives. The concept of being *Zen*, of completely and intentionally focusing on each act and experience in our lives, has become quite popular in the West. While some who attempt to follow these practices choose to explore the deep philosophies and traditions behind them, as with many popular trends, numerous followers acquire only a bumper sticker's worth of understanding. Regardless of practitioners' varying levels of knowledge or commitment, many people have become convinced *living in the now* is a good thing. Fear does not agree. Fear is not a fan of anything that teaches us to live in the present. Fear would rather we cast our gaze back and forth between resenting what went wrong in the past and dreading the potential disasters we can imagine happening in the future. Fear really likes it when we get so deeply into the rhythm of this repeating negative pattern that it becomes second nature to us.

When we look back towards the past, fear can ever

so helpfully use our emotions to skew our memories of what took place. We each remember past events from our own point of view. Consider how often the main character in a romantic comedy or horror film only knows part of what's going on. Perhaps everything the romantic lead can see seems to indicate that their love interest is being unfaithful. If the lead could see what the audience sees, they would realize their partner is actually dealing with an unfortunate medical problem or planning a loving surprise. We've all heard audiences yell, *Don't open that door!* to a character in a horror film. The audience can easily see the danger because it has more information. Each of us, similarly, is the lead character in our own life and can only remember the parts of the past we were aware of at the time. We may not have been privy to the unspoken thoughts of others or may have misread their motivations. Add our limited point of view to our tendency to cast the past in a negative light and we often end up with less than a complete picture of what happened.

The person we are now has undoubtedly had new experiences and matured or devolved in various ways. Looking back, from where we are now, on experiences that happened to younger versions of us has the potential to distort our view of

THE RIDE OF YOUR LIFE

certain aspects of the past. Fear can use these twisted recollections to convince us to lose hope and to believe our future is likely to be disappointing.

We begin to worry we will never again be able to have something we once had and lost, or to feel certain the things we desire will continue to elude us. Fear will encourage us to stay stuck between regretting or yearning for the past, and dreading what we may have to endure or miss in our future. Fear will most definitely try to get us to not live in the present.

Fear encourages us to find someone to blame for the unpleasant conditions of our lives, past and present. We may blame ourselves, others, or ping-pong between the two. If we choose to believe our life has always been, and most likely will always be unfair, we may feel trapped. In order to break this cycle of repeatedly using events from our past as evidence of a future guaranteed to be terrible, we need to do four things.

1. We need to have compassion for who we used to be.

We often judge our past selves based on who we are now. This isn't fair because the person we used to be didn't know as much as we know now. They were younger and less experienced.

2. We need to view everything in our lives as a learning experience.

This includes what happened in the past, what's currently happening, and what will happen in our future. Some of our best teachers are negative experiences and people who show us how we never want to be. Having what we don't want can teach us about what we do want. Think about choosing a new hat or suffering through a disastrous first date – we know when something isn't right for us. Figuring out why something is wrong for us helps us to identify what would fit more authentically into our lives. But in order to benefit from these negative examples we have to see them as opportunities to learn rather than as evidence we are failing or being shortchanged yet again.

3. We need to accept our current level of growth and evolution.

The opposite of failure isn't perfection, it is learning. We cannot learn from the lessons life offers us if we don't allow ourselves to make mistakes. If we focus our energy on figuring out who to blame for the negative situations in our lives we may miss the learning opportunities each experience offers us.

4. We need to grab joy whenever we can.

This is only possible if we notice and appreciate what is happening right here and right now. Getting angry when we make a wrong turn stops us from enjoying the scenery. Feeling afraid when we get lost keeps us from discovering new and interesting paths.

Remember: You can choose to enjoy the ride.

CHAPTER 5
The Perfect Pictures

THE RIDE OF YOUR LIFE

Most of us can clearly envision what our life would look like if everything were suddenly exactly the way we wish it would be. We have no trouble pixelating a fantasy photo with all the little details that would make our lives perfect. We know how many square feet and bedrooms our house would have. We can see ourselves enjoying the financial rewards and recognition from our dream career position. We can visualize the ideal romantic partner whose characteristics make them our perfect soul, body, and mind mate. Perhaps we have created a separate photo for each area of our lives: home, career, romantic partners, friends, prestige, and so on. The title of the photo album in our mind where we store these pictures may be something such as: *My Picture-Perfect Life* or *My Dream Life*.

There's nothing wrong with dreaming or having aspirations. Goals are useful. But many of us have created our perfect life images with such excruciating detail that we feel like failures if we don't acquire or achieve every single aspect of our perfect pictures. As you may imagine, fear is totally onboard with you feeling like a failure and will nudge you in this direction any time the opportunity presents itself. Feeling like a failure because our lives don't measure up to our preconceived and overly prescribed notion of perfection isn't good. What's just as bad, if not worse, are all the good things in our lives we miss when our eyes stay hyper-focused on our perfect pictures.

Many of us also create separate perfect pictures for our bodies and our emotional lives. Once again we use these pictures not as aspirations or representations of what we would like to journey towards but rather as a tool to measure our lack of success. We invite ourselves to feel like failures when we don't wear a certain size or lift a certain number of pounds. We may begin to find it difficult to be happy for friends or relatives who appear to reach one of the aspects of our imagined perfect picture if we haven't already achieved it for ourselves. It's not that we aren't happy for them. We are. It's just that their success casts such a strong light on our self-perceived failure.

We rewire our brains to label anything that doesn't exactly resemble our perfect pictures as unacceptable. If we can't acquire or achieve our imagined perfect life we may blame ourselves, our past, the Universe, or those who seem happier than us either in person or on social media. We may also be confused by people who are happy even though they don't have everything we have decided is necessary to live a perfect life. We assume they

THE RIDE OF YOUR LIFE   45

must be clueless or delusional. We may feel sorry for them or start to feel superior. Even if we feel bereft or devastated by what we don't have in our lives, at least we know what makes life good. Have you ever met someone and thought to yourself, *Wow, that person really gets it; they know what's important in life?* What you're actually saying is, *Wow, that person totally agrees with me about what's important in life.* Perhaps their perfect pictures, if they have them, look very similar to yours.

There's nothing wrong with *picturing* how we'd like our lives to go, but it can be really helpful to dig down and discover what is underneath or behind our definition of perfection. This can be much more useful than obsessing over the details. Imagine a friend comes to town and wants to go to an ice cream shop she read about in the *New York Times*. The shop is famous for its amazingly creamy ice cream. It also happens to offer some odd and interesting flavors. You and your friend drive downtown, park the car, and walk to the ice cream shop. There is a sign on the door: *Closed this week due to water leak.* Your friend is extremely disappointed. You name several other places in town that have really good ice cream. Your friend doesn't seem to be interested in any of your suggestions. You switch to pointing out carts that sell fabulous gelato and handmade ices. Your friend says no to all of these.

You assumed your friend's perfect dessert, based on their description of the *Times* article, was a dish of high quality ice cream. This is why you started listing other places to get quality ice cream and other frozen desserts. But what your friend really wanted was to try something unusual, similar to the odd and interesting ice cream flavors mentioned in the *Times* article. Your friend didn't care as much about having ice cream or something cold; they wanted to try something out of the ordinary. If you had realized this, you could have taken them to the pastry shop with the chocolate bacon cupcakes.

Sometimes we are just as clueless about what is underneath our own perfect pictures. Often our perfect picture turns out to be just one possible manifestation of what we want. Something else could fulfill our desires just as well or even better if we truly understood why we want what we want. Consider attempting to discover the why behind each of your perfect pictures. Once you figure out how to define your desires in a way that doesn't limit you to one specific way to fulfill them, you can begin to rethink your aspirations. Which ones do you want to keep as they are? Which ones do you want to alter to include other ways of being

THE RIDE OF YOUR LIFE

fulfilled? Which ones are not only too limited but are also based on something you realize isn't actually important to you now, even if it used to be?

Maybe your original perfect picture was of you wearing a certain size of clothing. You believed this would make you attractive to others. Recently, you've discovered what you really want is to be healthy and strong, and to feel good about yourself. Maybe size will no longer be the goal. Instead, you'll focus on how you feel in your body, and how much strength and stamina you have. Chances are if you feel good in your body, others will appreciate how you look. If they don't appreciate you when you feel good about yourself maybe they're using their own perfect pictures as criteria for judging you unfairly. Explore your perfect pictures to discover what brings you joy. Stop looking for narrow results. Start figuring out what you really want.

Remember: Perfect pictures can be out of focus.

CHAPTER 6
The Face-to-face

THE RIDE OF YOUR LIFE

One of the necessary ingredients for developing the ability to use fear as a helpful tool in your life is a deep understanding of the complex make-up of your particular version of fear. This is next to impossible to achieve if you repeatedly choose to pretend your fear doesn't exist or try to hide from it. It also won't happen if you develop a habit of fearfully (ironic) telling fear to, *Shut up and leave me alone!* You need to get to know your fear, but simply listening to what your fear tells you won't automatically provide any helpful insights. Hanging out with friends, listening to their opinions, and hearing about their experiences, usually helps us to know them better. However, if a friend is a drama queen, or a rabid doom and gloom forecaster, or seems to live to get a rise out of us, chances are we won't necessarily get much insight into what is going on for them at a deeper level by simply spending time with them. We would probably get to witness their habits and tendencies, but these behaviors may merely be self-protective barriers or self-promoting posturing rather than a reflection of who our friend really is inside.

Imagine you are trying to get to know a friend who fits this description. How might you go about getting to know the real person underneath all of their shenanigans? You'd probably have to begin by making sure your friend feels safe and at ease. If they detect even a hint of the possibility of you judging them, they will most likely close down and refuse to let you in. This could manifest as a stubborn and possibly curt refusal to continue the conversation. They might choose to stomp off without saying another word or spew a vitriolic description of your jerkitude before storming off. So yeah, comfort is key.

You need to actually refrain from judging them not just *hide* your judgment from them. You need to be clear in your own mind about why you want to get to the bottom of their behaviors. Check your intentions. Do you really want a better relationship with this person or do you secretly want to demonstrate you are superior in some way? Your friend will pick up on your true feelings whether you yourself are aware of them or not.

Finally, bring a healthy dose of compassion with you. This will go a long way toward warding off judgment, as judgment and compassion have difficulty occupying the same space. Remember, the experiences your friend has had have helped to bring them to where they are now. Some of these things may have happened to them when they were younger and less capable. Realize you don't know what kind of support they did or didn't

THE RIDE OF YOUR LIFE

have along the way. You may also be unaware of the effectiveness of their current support network.

Realize it will most likely take multiple conversations for them to trust you enough to open up completely. Be patient. This is a process not an errand to go out and accomplish when you have a few minutes. Start by doing more listening than talking. Ask a few open-ended and obviously non-judgmental questions. Help them see the causality links between their responses to past incidents in their lives and their current behaviors. Invite your friend to consider alternative viewpoints if they seem receptive. Don't assign blame. Don't label them as stupid or unfortunate.

Now let's get back to attempting this same process with your fear. Imagine metaphorically taking your fear out for a cup of coffee or an adult beverage in order to get to know it. Talking to your fear is similar to being in the middle of one of your dreams. It's not that the situation isn't real but rather that it is symbolic and representative of your life – and here's the kicker – we are often *all* the characters in our dreams. In reality we are what is underneath our fear. Our reactions to our life experiences create our fear. We must make ourselves feel comfortable and not judged in order to have the courage to dig into why our fear acts as it does. We must refrain from labeling ourselves as stupid or as a hapless victim. We must have compassion for ourselves as we talk to our fear to understand how it came to be as it is now. We must invite ourselves to begin to see and consider alternate viewpoints. We must own up to our part in the causality of our circumstances. We must be patient with ourselves and intentionally choose to celebrate each small spurt of personal growth that moves us forward.

Remember: We are the architects of our own fear.

CHAPTER 7
The Avoidance

THE RIDE OF YOUR LIFE

Our culture puts a heavy emphasis on happy endings. We are urged to settle for nothing less than perfection in our lives. Many of us exert copious amounts of energy to avoid any potentially uncomfortable situation. We worry our feelings of discomfort and dissatisfaction signal a failure on our part to achieve the happiness and success expected of us. We are convinced others aren't as uncomfortable in their lives as we are. Social media shows us slice after slice of the perfect lives others seem to effortlessly create and enjoy. It's easy for us to compare and to find ourselves (and our lives) lacking.

Fear reinforces these self-judgments and invites us to spiral into feelings of overwhelming helplessness. On the outside we seem to be accomplishing the necessary tasks of our daily lives, but inside we may feel like an astronaut whose cord to the mother ship has been cut: drifting with no chance of rescue. When this happens, fear offers a steady stream of statements and questions designed to freak us out. Think a Greek chorus intoning warnings of tragedy, or dystopian horror movie trailers. If we buy into the negative litany fear offers we may continue to sink further and further into the *why-me* muck of despair. Sometimes we try to run. Sometimes we try to hide. Neither of these usually works.

When our attempt to close our ears to fear's drone of destructive head-tweets doesn't work, we may seek comfort by overindulging. We jump feet first into a distraction: sex, sloth, substances, exercise, cleaning, anything we think is powerful enough to overwrite and thus block out the negative messages. But we cannot run from ourselves – we're still there wherever we are. Choosing to focus on doing something else while secretly trying to outrun these messages doesn't work. Avoidance isn't the answer.

We do, however, need to take a break when we get caught up in this cyclone of cacophony. We *do* need to interrupt the pattern. How is taking a break different than avoidance? Aren't we still trying to avoid our feelings? Not if we choose to purposely acknowledge the torrent of negativity fear is pouring into our heads before shifting our focus to another activity. Not if we slow down and tell ourselves something that sounds a bit like this: *I need a few minutes right now. I need to distract myself so I can collect myself. I'm not avoiding what I'm feeling; I'm interrupting the flow hoping to lower the volume and slow down the frequency. When I return to face my feelings I will try to improve the reception so I can hear any bits of truth hiding among the lies and exaggerations. I will not allow my unwillingness to experience discomfort to keep me from learning from my feelings.*

Fear is an expert at taking a tiny, innocuous thing and building into something huge and horrible. A sneeze becomes the flu. A pimple turns into a rare disease. A look transforms into a death threat, a smile into a sinister secret, a worry into a shattered life. We need to reach down and find our powers of logic, our experiential knowledge, our intuition, and our instincts. These innate and learned abilities can help us to locate the more realistic and appropriately sized information hiding within the dystopian panorama fear offers us. There will undoubtedly be aspects of fear's message we are not yet ready to confront. If we acknowledge them and label them for *future review*, we can turn their insistent yammering to a dull hum we can live with until we are ready to go back and explore further. Fear hopes we won't do this, because if we do, there's less of a chance we will panic and be at the mercy of our worst expectations. Fear wants us to believe there are only three ways to respond to something that frightens us:

1. run like hell with no guarantee we'll get away

2. do battle and most likely lose

3. surrender and be destroyed

But there is a fourth choice: to parley, to engage in a discussion with the opposing side. On one side is: you – as fear paints you to be; and on the other side is: you – as you authentically are (and can be) when you refuse to buy into fear's lies. Each side agrees to remain civil as they discuss their individual needs and attempt to dispel each other's misconceptions. You will undoubtedly feel vulnerable and exposed during these talks. You will also have the opportunity to learn where to draw effective boundaries. Fear cannot be annihilated but it can be understood. If we are willing to parley with our fear we have the potential to discover the source of the dark shadows fear offers. Because we are the architects of our fears, we can get access to the blueprints. These insights can help us figure out how to choose to dwell in the light.

Remember: Sometimes a little discomfort can be a good thing.

CHAPTER 8
The Set-up

THE RIDE OF YOUR LIFE

Sometimes we unintentionally choose to live in the shadows projected by our fear. We do this by maintaining an environment where it is easy for our fear to flourish. We start by spending an inordinate amount of our time attempting to prove our fears are realistic. We mischaracterize situations to ourselves and to others and present them as evidence of the legitimacy of our fears. We carefully choose words and actions designed to support our unsubstantiated hysteria. We operate in a state of emotional empiricism, but instead of thinking: *I'll believe it when I see it*, we subconsciously think: *I'll only allow myself to see evidence I can twist to justify my fears*. We refuse to acknowledge any evidence disproving or challenging the scary realities our fear offers us. We become so invested in being right we continue to automatically misunderstand, and subsequently mislabel, whatever happens in our lives as further proof of the dark pictures we fear.

We worry a lot about something happening unexpectedly that we won't be able to handle. We feel more comfortable knowing what's going to happen even if we are in a negative situation stuck on repeat. Our life may be shit but it's our shit. It's familiar and there's a security in this familiarity. Meanwhile we continue to villainize others or blame the Universe for the less than stellar conditions of our lives. We may become angry or devastated by what we perceive as our unending victimhood. We begin to do the emotional Hokey Pokey of complaining: *We put our righteous blame right in the way of seeing what's right in front of us; we take our it's-not-right-I'm-always-a-victim right out on our self-esteem; we put our what-right-does-the-Universe-have-to-treat-me-this-way in the way of our own growth; then we shake ourselves right out of the reality of our lives.* When we do this dance long enough, our anger and despair about our lives become our lives. We have no idea who we are without all our drama and feelings of devastation. Fear, true to form, tells us it would be too scary to find out who we are underneath our own uproar.

We express a desire for change but our choices continue to entrench us ever more deeply into a state of avoidance. We believe, either consciously or subconsciously, that facing our fear would leave us naked in an emotional desert with no idea of how to get what we need to survive. We are addicted to needing to know what's going to happen next. We may not like the way our lives are but at least our lives are predictable. *Besides,* we argue, *we have tried to change things in the past and it never works.* Of course it doesn't, not when we attempt to change things only to prove they are impossible to change.

THE RIDE OF YOUR LIFE

We don't like what we have but we want to be excused from taking a chance at trying for something else. That would involve looking to see what is underneath our fear and we are afraid of what we may find there. *What if I am worse or more pathetic than other people? What if I'm inept and incapable of ever taking charge of my life?* We all have darkness and light. Whatever your level and brand of darkness, it probably won't earn you any gold evil medals or incite a mob to run you out of town. Only characters in fairytales, comics, poorly written novels, and subpar movies are inherently all-good or all-bad. Balance, comfort, and peace are not based on certainty or on things being Disney-endings perfect. Instead they come from being aware and intentional about the choices we make: what we choose to say to ourselves and to others, and which actions we choose to take.

We must be aware of why we say and do what we do. Are we trying to maintain outdated defensive mechanisms that worked or seemed to work when we were younger? Are we trying to prove we can't win because we are afraid we will fail? Are we attempting to prove no one will ever love us because we are afraid we are truly unlovable? All emotions are part of the fabric of life. What we call a bad day is very much like a good day: simply an opportunity to choose how to respond, to learn about what scares us, and to purposely choose to accept our current feelings while trying to build greater understanding and compassion for ourselves and eventually for others as well. Meanwhile fear whispers in our ears and tells us to protect ourselves from life. Fear offers to stand outside the barricaded doors of our hearts ready to identify and repel those who would harm us. It invites us to be spectators instead of participants, to keep our lives tuned to the same channel playing the same soap opera over and over again.

Fear congratulates us when we rage against the circumstances of our lives and tells us we're smart when we cower, too afraid to take chances. It encourages us to reinforce our emotional muscle memories based on ineffectual old patterns and crusty, moldy doubts. Fear tells us to reject anything that doesn't fit our rationalization for why things are as they are in our lives. We are invited to build up our defenses so we don't have to feel the feelings we don't want to feel. But these defenses also act as a barrier that keeps us from accessing our self-awareness and the ability to connect to others. We end up alone even when surrounded by a cheering squad of friends who agree with our fear-distorted view of the world.

Even if we begin to suspect our defense mechanisms are ineffective, we may still hesitate to try something new. *What if it doesn't work? I'll feel like such an idiot if I find out I wasted so much time living my life based on lies.* There is also a part of us that realizes we cannot pick up a new way of functioning in the world without first setting down the old way. Think of the way you operate in the world as a bag of life tools. You can't pick up of new bag of tools until you put the old bag down on the floor. Can you see the moment just after you set down the old bag of tools? In that moment *before* you pick up the new bag, your hands will be empty. This can be the scariest thing of all. But if the old bag affects our life in negative ways, if it harms us, we need to put it down. It takes bravery to let go of something you have become used to, even if it is something you no longer want, even if it harms you.

Here's a classic example of our human tendency to hold on to old patterns. Imagine a first-year college student, Ali, who complains to friends about getting calls from home almost every day. Ali's parents want to make sure Ali is happy and adjusting to being away from home. Ali tells them there is no need to call so often. Eventually Ali's parents start calling only on Sundays. The conversations are just as friendly and loving as ever; however, Ali complains to friends about receiving fewer calls from home. Ali has no real reason to be upset but nevertheless continues to feel uncomfortable. The first steps of change can often feel this way.

Remember: Don't focus on what you don't want.

CHAPTER 9
The Rejection

THE RIDE OF YOUR LIFE

Every once in a while, someone reaches out and tries to help us when they see us overcome by fear. Most of the time we welcome sympathy or empathy but reject suggestions for alternate ways to look at our situation. Even when we say we want to be rescued from what's happening in our lives, we may still take offense if someone suggests slowing down and exploring our situation more deeply to understand it better. We adamantly defend our right to live within our misery. *Who do they think they are? They say they care but all they do is judge me. They have absolutely no idea what I'm going through. They don't understand how trapped I am.* We believe we are refusing to accept misinterpretations of our situation offered by those who obviously, at least to us, don't understand it. We may complain about our serially cheating lover whom we believe will never change; yet, we also say we don't want to imagine our world without them. We whine about the horrible ways they treat us but refuse to perceive their actions as abusive. We also refuse to entertain the possibility that our current partner may not be a good match for us. We want everyone in our support network to acknowledge how miserable our situation is, but if anyone suggests it may be time to move on, we vehemently defend our partner and explain how we could never get anyone else to love us.

We've created a perfect trap for ourselves without realizing the full extent of the trap's ability to do us harm. When others show us potential ways to free ourselves, we hesitate, afraid of the pain and discomfort freedom may cause. They reassure us we'll heal once we escape, but we're not so sure. *If I walk away I'll be alone. I'll have no one. At least I have someone now. There are a lot of jerks out there. I don't know if I could get anyone else to love me.*

Maybe life with our partner or at our job is actually pretty wonderful but we find ourselves waiting nervously for it to blow up or disappear. *This can't possibly last. It feels too good to be true. I'm bound to screw it up eventually, and if I don't, my partner (or boss) probably will.* We worry hidden issues will come to light and disenchantment will descend. Of course this keeps us from enjoying what we have but *better safe than sorry*. We believe we must remain vigilant to avoid the pain of getting blindsided. Fear grins smugly in the background, as we pre-inhabit our worst-case scenarios without realizing that's what we're doing. We don't appreciate it when others try to point out what's happening. *What do they know? They're not living my life.* True enough, but what are we missing in our current lives while our eyes stay fixed on potential

THE RIDE OF YOUR LIFE

disaster? Does our hyper-focus on what we fear have the power to increase its chances of happening?

Sometimes we commiserate with people who are in situations similar to ours. We reinforce each other's victim mentality and encourage hyper-vigilance. Other times we are amazed by how someone else doesn't seem to appreciate how good their current situation is, or we are appalled by a friend choosing to stay in an impossible romantic or work situation. We get really upset when they don't take our advice. We marvel at their blindness, their stubbornness, and their poor choices. We become hurt or angry when they tell us we're clueless and interfering. We don't notice our own behaviors being mirrored back to us. But our subconscious sees what our conscious mind refuses to acknowledge. It screams at us to recognize ourselves in our friends' behaviors, to learn from the familiar negative examples on display.

The anger and frustration we feel toward our supposedly misguided friends may actually be a manifestation of our anger at ourselves. One part of us realizes the loop we've locked ourselves into while another part cannot push this realization away fast enough. We continue to reject learning from the behaviors of our wayward friends and to refuse the helpful guidance offered by well-meaning friends.

We deny the possibility of success because we are convinced we will fail. We don't believe we can escape our own misfortune; therefore, it feels too scary to try. We are afraid to hope. If we refuse to choose change, we are choosing, by default, to support what currently exists. This guarantees a continuation of more of what we don't want.

We surround ourselves with people who reinforce our perceptions. They tell us we are brave to stick it out even though our situation is so difficult, or wise to distrust what appears to be happiness. We misread and mislabel the words and actions of our lovers, friends, coworkers, or bosses to prove the dystopian future we fear. We make choices that invite others to behave the way we fear they will behave. We begin to craft and cause what we fear. With our eyes glued to our emotional horizon we nervously anticipate the approach of the joy-sucking zombies in our lives and fail to notice our own self-defeating behaviors.

Remember: Stop dancing so fast and look in the mirror.

CHAPTER 10
The What if?

THE RIDE OF YOUR LIFE

Fear often uses what if questions to scare us. *What if they find out I'm not as good as they think I am? What if they don't believe me? What if they leave me?* But we can construct better *what if* questions for ourselves. We can choose to stop obsessing about what we are afraid *might* happen. We can decide to stop seeing innocent events in our lives as further proof of what we fear.

Imagine you return to your car in a parking lot and discover someone has sideswiped the front door on the driver's side. There are telltale bits of red paint in the scratches and small depressions on the car door. Maybe the other driver was a jerk and rode off knowing what they did. Maybe they were oblivious because their music was cranked and they were distracted. It doesn't really matter. Your car is damaged and so is your equilibrium. Your first reaction may be a haze of anger or a defeated shoulder-slump of *Why does this kind of stuff always seem to happen to me?*

These are fairly common first-reactions; however, if you stay in one of these negative headspaces you will probably start to ask yourself worry causing what if questions. *What if this is too expensive to fix? What if my insurance doubles? What if this reduces the resale value of my car? What if my significant other thinks*

I'm an idiot? What if this keeps happening to me? You may continue to experience these negative emotions as you obsess over the scrape-and-run for days. You may unintentionally end up using these revisited, incident-related feelings as an accelerant to stoke the fires of unrelated, former feelings of discontent or despair.

>CUT! Stop everything.

What if you accepted your negative feelings not as evidence that the scary things you want to avoid are true – *your life isn't good enough, or fair, or ever going to change* – but instead simply allowed yourself to feel all your feelings deeply, even the scary ones? What if you chose to feel compassion for yourself and for every other parker of cars who has returned to a scrape-and-run? What if you chose to focus on the practical choices you had to make? *Should you get the car fixed? Should you call your insurance company or not?* What if you paused to ask yourself if *you* would leave a note containing your contact information if you ever slightly crunched someone else's car when no one was around to witness the incident? And what if this discovery process really was only about self-discovery and not about self-judgment?

THE RIDE OF YOUR LIFE

What if you thought about the scrape-and-run as just one more moment in your story? Not a moment representing how crappy or out of control your life seems to be, but rather just one of the many moments that make up your life. And what if you saw yourself as acceptable right now, without being hypercritical of all your feelings and tendencies and choices? What if you didn't give this less-than-desirable and definitely annoying moment the power to help fear gain even more control of your life?

And what if you allowed yourself to not be very good at doing this the first time you tried? What if you understood you were just beginning to attempt to do things a new way in your life? What if you didn't lose your commitment and resolve to try to live life differently just because you weren't perfect? What if you realized being less than perfect didn't make you a failure?

What if you imagined what you would say to yourself and to others about the scrape-and-run, if you were living your life with acceptance of wherever you happened to be in your emotional journey? What if the expression on your face and the way you held and moved your body reflected a belief that a scrape-and-run doesn't have the power to create feelings of dread or despair? What if the scrape-and-run only unsettled you initially but then you didn't accept the invitation to feel overly angry or sad?

What if you tried to inhabit your inspirational life now while simultaneously accepting your current levels of growth and awareness? What if you slowed down and looked at the dark pictures fear feeds you and realized they are gunk-filled filters clouding your perception of reality? What if you also resisted the temptation to pretend everything was wonderful in order to keep yourself from facing and exploring your fears? What if you mined the useful nuggets from the negative offerings fear continuously delivers and said no thank you to the rest? What if you sought out and surrounded yourself with friends who also wanted to try to do this?

What if you didn't feel distain for, or superior to, those who choose to stay stuck where you used to be? What if you were willing to get the equivalent of emotionally scraped knees and muddy shoes while you were learning a different way to be? And what if you, more often than not, refused to see these occurrences as failures or as evidence of the futility of trying to change? What if you cut yourself a break? What if you cut others a break too but RSVP-ed, *not attending* to any invitations they offered to

THE RIDE OF YOUR LIFE

join them on the dark side?

What if you chose to live, to laugh, to love? What if you chose to take chances instead of to hide from an imagined less-than-satisfying life?

Remember: Use your energy to create self-awareness instead of fear.

Check out Cinse's online companion workshop filled with strategies and techniques at:
udemy.com/the-ride-of-your-life.

Use SEECHOOSEDO1 for a discounted price.

ABOUT THE AUTHOR

Cinse Bonino is a former professor of Creativity & Conceptual Development with a background in Education and the Psychology of Human Learning. Cinse currently presents workshops and talks on: creativity, problem solving, communication, teaching and learning, and personal awareness. She also does one-on-one awareness sessions (in person and online) to help individuals better define and create the way they want to be in the world. Cinse lives in Burlington, Vermont, with her cats Jasper and Melina, and enjoys widely spaced but deeply appreciated visits from her son who currently serves in the U. S. Army.
Check out Cinse's offerings at:
seechoosedo.com

Special thanks to
Lindsey Rae for an eagle eye and open heart,
to Paul for generous unwavering belief,
to Cate Lowman for all the golden nuggets,
and to the home team at Phoenix Books in
Burlington, Vermont

Deep thanks to my father for always tossing
wisdom in my direction

*Cover art & design and book layout by the
fabulously talented Mollie Coons
molliecoons.com*

www.ingramcontent.com/pod-product-compliance
Lightning Source LLC
Chambersburg PA
CBHW050544300426
44113CB00012B/2249